L. Banta

"Be Holy..."

(1st Peter 1:16)

But don't start thinking like you're

"ALL THAT" and better than me.

WHAT TO DO AND SAY TO THESE DIFFICULT

PEOPLE WITHOUT LOSING YOUR COOL AND

STARTING A FIGHT

CHAPTERS

<u>Self – Pride Vs. Humility</u>

Have you ever known a difficult Christian? (I'll be nice and call them difficult for now). Yes, they exist, and they are in our midst everyday…in our churches, our workplaces, and even in our own families. Difficult Christians are those who are so religious, that they scare away the very people they are supposed to help. Instead of living testimonies, they are living accusers, and in their arrogance, they blame others for not being like them.

"I saw him at the store yesterday… yeah, he was walking in the beer aisle. I didn't see him leave, but he was in there for a long time. I'll betcha… he's drinking again… and he's supposed to be a Christian? I don't even walk PAST that aisle."

They're just too judgmental.

These types of Christians try to convict us in every way as if we are not as Christian as them or not as *saved* as they are. You know the types; those who can quote scripture at the drop of a hat, not the ones in the bible, but the ones that *sound* like those in the bible. They don't quote from the book of Genesis, but from the book of *"General-sayings."* They don't know the book of Acts, but they *act* like they know the book. They will say something like,

"Girl… the bible says, It is what it is."

No, it doesn't… that is nowhere in the bible. Teach them how *that saying* is <u>man-made</u> and it means "there is no hope of changing things." They need to know that the bible says in Mark 10:27,

"With men it is impossible, but not with God, for with God, all things are possible."

But they have no problem about letting us know that we are less Godly than they are, because we don't go to *"their"* church. They walk around with their heads in the clouds, chanting… not singing, and praying just to put their religion on display. These difficult Christians are the ones that no one wants to invite to the community picnic, or the family reunion, because they make it hard for everyone else to enjoy each other… and it seems like they always wanna be in the spotlight praying for you. You know… they'll grab your hands very quickly.

You may say, *"I've got a throbbing headache."*

The next thing you know… they've grabbed your hands and are pulling you to the side trying to heal you just so they can have the bragging rights in front of the crowd. They don't care if you're eating, if you've got barbecue sauce on your hands, or if you're holding a puppy. They probably *mean* well, but their need for fame is so great that they wanna pray for you so everyone can see that they're *all that*. To them… it's their power not God's, and they're holier than you. They need to be reminded that Jesus tells us,

"When you pray, don't be like the hypocrites who love to pray publicly on street corners and in the synagogues where everyone can see them. I tell you the truth; that is all the reward they will ever get." (Mathew 6:5) N.L.T.

Just thank them and tell them that you prefer to pray for yourself. The reward that they get is in their own proud minds as they show-off in their arrogance.

There is a difference between being religious and being spiritual. A religious Christian lives by traditions given to them by past habits and rules of the church of which they attend. A spiritual Christian lives by the word of God, without following traditions of any church, but by every word that proceeds out of the mouth of God (Matthew 4:4), by the Holy Spirit.

By keeping a humble character, we can coexist in the world without chasing everyone away. However, there are some difficult Christians who seem too elevated for us *common folks down here in the hood* and unapproachable just because of who they are.

You know that type? They act like Saint *Karen* of *"Uppity Ave.*, or Bishop Tyrone from the Eastside Church of *"High Incomes Only."*

As Christians, we do not have to flaunt who we are, but instead, let our spirituality and righteousness show itself in the way we live. In this way, others will come to us on their own with opportunities for us to tell them about the joy of the Lord.

<u>**Boasting vs. Testimony**</u>

Have you ever been around someone who just drains your energy, constantly bragging on themselves? They seem to go on and on about their favorite subject…themselves. In the world of *religion*, there are Christians like that too. These types of Christians may mean well, but they try our nerves to the extreme. These types of Christians go on and on so much about what they have received from God, that they take away the hope that anyone else may have of receiving from God. Instead of lifting brothers and sisters in Christ, they make it depressing to hear them brag and boast about their blessings. They're like:

"I was praying to God, right? Then I walked down the street and found $20, aint God good? So, I played my number, right? Then I hit for $2000, aint he

good? So, I was looking for a car, right? Then I ran into

this guy from church who was selling his car for $1000,

but I prayed, and he sold it to me for $800, won't he do

it? So, I put $200 in the tank and drove that car to

Florida and found a job as soon as I got there, aint God

good? Then I prayed and the job paid for me an

apartment… aint he good? I'm just here to get my stuff

because God moved me to Florida, and I just know he's

gonna make me rich."

You know them? They make God sound like their personal magician or something. All that happened to them might be true, but they cause us to question ourselves and question God…

"Why didn't I get blessed like that? What am I doing wrong? Are they better than me? God, do you love them more than me?

They make us feel as if we are doing something wrong… and cause us to wonder what's the use in trying to be a good Christian.

We are to *testify* of what God has done in our life, without sounding inflated and boastful. We want to encourage, not discourage others. The bible says…

"*…Be ready always to give an answer to every man that asketh you a reason of the hope that is in you with meekness and fear.*" (1 Peter 3:15).

This means for us to use our testimonies as *answers* to *questions* that someone may ask us concerning how we got where we are with God, and not for boasting. The reason for the hope within us may be the things of which we have to testify. The scripture says to give these answers with *"meekness and fear"* which is humility and respect, and not bold bragging.

So overly focused on what God has done for them, these boastful Christians have forgotten the reason why he has. Patiently remind those types of Christians that God blesses us for us to use those blessings *to give him glory* and *to be a blessing to others* in whatever way we are called, according to his purpose. (Romans 8:28). In doing this, we are *building up* hope in others, rather than tearing it down.

Conceited vs. Humble

Have you ever known someone who, according to themselves, knows everything about everything? These types of people are very difficult to deal with because they leave no room for the opinions or ideas of others. Whatever the discussion or subject, they always seem to have been there and done that and claim to have the answer to everything. They rarely give anyone a chance to even talk, much less make suggestions about anything. These people pretend to be leaders, but they only crave the attention and status that their showboating intelligence brings. There are Christians who have this type of character as well.

I have a cousin like that. Love him to no end… but he thinks he is a walking bible encyclopedia. We used to have these bible studies once a month and he would always be the one who wanted to tell a bible

fact… only his facts were wrong. At one of those

meetings, he told us…

"You know the reason Jesus turned the glass of

water into wine?" It was because they ran out of the

grapes that they needed to make more and they didn't

have any refrigerators back then, so they had to use cold

water from the well in the ground, then cover it with

cloth in the shade to keep it cool."

Christians like that can turn any subject into a lie

and make others believe it! (First, it wasn't a glass of

water Jesus turned into wine, it was six stone jars

according to John 2:1-11).

He has plenty of nonfactual stories like that, but I

will never embarrass him, I just let him tell his stories.

That's how you must handle someone like that…

especially with the older Christians. They can be great

charismatic actors who win the "Grammy" every time

the curtain rises.

The bible says… *"Be not wise in thine own

eyes..."* (Proverbs 3:7).

This means for us not to think of ourselves as all

knowing because of our life experiences and testimonies

or what you *think* you know. No one knows everything.

We should remember that there is always room for us to

learn and grow from others. The way one person

perceives a situation may be completely different from

the way another person will see it. It is the same way

with an answer. One person's solution may not be the

right one for another person. Again… "No one knows

everything."

The word of God says… *"There is more hope for fools than for people who think they are wise."* (Proverbs 26:12 NLT).

This means, that conceit, closes our mind to learning new things, and even a fool is open to receive teaching. As we endeavor to tell others about God's grace, we need to be willing to be humbled so that in doing so, we do not appear full of ourselves, but full of the Holy Spirit.

Hindering vs. Helping

"What sorrow awaits you teachers of religious law and you Pharisees. Hypocrites! For you shut the door of the Kingdom of Heaven in people's faces. You won't go in yourselves, and you don't let others enter either." (Matthew 23:13 NIV).

That was Jesus who was concerned about the way the Pharisees were treating other people. Unfortunately, there are Christians who are very much like that today. They still practice religious law (the Ten Commandments) and condemn others for not being able to keep them, when they themselves cannot keep them. These types of Christians hinder us from learning the truth of the gospel, and from receiving true salvation through Christ Jesus our Lord and Savior. Instead of aiding us in our journey to righteousness, they undermine us and make us feel as if we are less than able

to enter Gods wonderful grace. They pretend to be better

than us, as if they are on a higher plane of existence.

They say things like…

"I pray six times a day and never miss church."

Well, that's good for you. That's wonderful, but

people have different things going on in their lives.

Everyone can't do that, so don't make people feel less of

a Christian or of a person than you.

Matthew 23:12 says, *"For whoever exalts himself

shall be humbled, and whoever humbles himself will be

exalted."* (NIV).

Suggest to those types of Christians that by not judging

others, but by *teaching and helping*, we can uplift them

in a humble way and inspire them to understand the

grace and righteousness of God with integrity and patience. Because when we judge others arrogantly, we belittle ourselves and portray a lie about Christianity to others.

Jesus said that these type of hypocrites… "…*clean out the outside of the cup and dish, but inside they are full of greed and self-indulgence.*" (Matthew 23:25 NIV).

That means that we need to stop playing church by dressing the part and *appearing* to be holy, by really examine ourselves within. As Christians, before we try to tell someone else how wrong they are living, we need to judge the way we are living our own lives.

<u>Self-righteous vs. Righteous self</u>

The dictionary defines self-righteousness as being confident of one's own righteousness, especially when smugly moralistic and intolerant of the opinions and behavior of others.

The bible says… *"There is a generation that are pure in their own eyes, and yet is not washed from their filthiness."* (Proverbs 30:12).

In the world, there are these types of Christians who think that they are so high and mighty, that none of us *ordinary* Christians are worthy to be in their presence. They see us as ordinary because they are uppity and egotistical, precious in their own minds and too good to associate with non-believers, or even other believers.

These pretentious Christians, easily recognized by their trademark attitudes, are among us today…

"Girl, I got blessed with $200 so you know I'm going shopping. I'll donate something to the homeless shelter next time. I gotta catch that sale today… it's the last day! Those people get on my nerves anyway. They're not giving ME nothing"

You've heard them before. They are out for themselves and ignore the needs of others. They have enough to help, but help no one, not even their own families. They are even selfish with God and refuse to share the gospel for fear that others may receive more blessings than they have. They show partiality to people, and only show love to those whom they have judged worthy of their time and energy.

The bible says… *"Do not think of yourself more highly than you ought, but rather think of yourself with sober judgment, in accordance with the measure of faith that God has given you.* (Romans 12:3 NIV).

We are to *judge ourselves*, not compare ourselves to others by the things we have acquired. Carefully remind those selfish Christians to judge themselves according to the amount of faith they have within. Christians must look deep within our hearts and ask ourselves... *"Am I really being the type of Christian that God wants me to be?"*

Galatians 6:3 says, *"For if a man thinks of himself to be something, when he is nothing, he deceiveth himself."*

Conformed Vs. Transformed

Conforming to the world means to give in to its shallow and self-centered ideals. The world believes that its way of life is superior to the standards of living set before us in the word of God. Simply put… the world doesn't care what the bible says. To the world…

"It's all about getting that money, makin that cheddar, and blowin up! It's all about my whip, my crib, and my sexiness."

The world wants us to be just like that. To be clear… when I refer to the "world," I'm referring to its character, its thinking, and the emphasis on flesh… the way everything kinda revolves around sex and money out there. I've seen people who I know are Christians, just sell out themselves to the world for money and fame by being sexy and immoral.

I know an entertainer who grew up in the church, sang in the choir, father was a pastor, family practically ran the church, but now that entertainer has won a Grammy for the sexiest video of the year by selling out for fame and personal glory. It happened. Is that how we're supposed to use God's blessing? What do we do?

Conforming to the world means to give in to what we see and hear in the media. With technology today, the world can show us sexy images on computers right in our pockets. TV screens are constantly enticing us and reminding us of our bodily shortcomings. The world tells us that we are not good enough in the way that we are… not cute enough, not manly enough, not athletic enough, not smart enough; It makes us dissatisfied with ourselves and creates the desire to look and be like the images that we see.

- *"If you buy this diet, you can be beautiful in just 30 days."*

- *"Eating this brand of food will make you feel like you're floating on a cloud."*

- *Drinking this flavor of beer will really get your party started."*

- *This breakthrough pill will make you look ten years younger and sexy again."*

The world tells and shows us that drugs can make us feel better, causing us to think that we are not as happy as we can be. That tricky information depresses many people, causing a desire to conform to that drug-world, to feel like, look like, and be like the people they see on the screens. The world shows us other people who look like us, as they drink and party, which gives us the illusion that our own lives are mundane and boring so we must conform to drinking and partying to have exciting lives like theirs.

Let's face it… the world is also full of sex and extramarital affairs which is glamorized in the media, causing people to assume that it is fine and even adventurous to go get a girlfriend or boyfriend even though you're married. There are pictures, images and movies that portray it as exciting or even justified. The world's sex industry grosses 13 billion dollars a year in the United States alone.

My point is…. God is not found in any of these claims, yet the world tells us to *"come do this;*

Everybody's doin it… be free, be like everyone else, be like us, we're better than everyone… but we're just havin fun."

The sad thing is that there are so-called Christians who condone these things and this way of life. They believe that it is fine to live this way, as they go to church, and pay their respects to God. They believe that makes it okay, and they have no problem with doing it.

- *"I'm wearin my new outfit to church today because after the service, I'm gotta stop at the club. I gotta get there to meet that promoter from Detroit and I wanna look cute, fine, and sexy. I know he wants me, but don't tell my husband."*

- *"Yeah... I gotta sneak outta church early today. I'm meetin sister Smith at the club and I gotta wash my car. She thinks I'm a promoter from Detroit, and she wants me. But don't tell my wife."*

Those types of Christians need to know that although we are no longer under the law, and Christ died for our sins, we cannot use this as a reason for, or an excuse to conform to the world's ways. By renewing our minds, we *transform* into the way and lifestyle of Christ and learn to overcome the influences and the temptations of the world. (Romans 12:2). We learn the word of God, and transform into his marvelous light, which gives us a more fulfilling, enjoyable life, for we are *in* the world, but we do not have to be part *of* it.

Jesus says in John 15:18-19… *"If the world hates you, ye know that it hated me before it hated you. If ye were of the world, the world would love his own: but because ye are not of the world, but I have chosen you out of the world, therefore the world hateth you."*

- We are constructed or born into the world.

- We are reconstructed or born again into Christ.

- We are changed into the worldly man.

- When we believe in Christ, we exchange the worldly man for the spiritual man.

- In the world, we are made.

- In Christ, we are created.

We should not be like hypocrites, demonstrating the traits and ways of the world, yet still calling ourselves Christians. We should not act as if we are better than anyone else. We do not have to be like those artificial Christians with their sanctimonious attitudes. They are egotistical about God, with their noses in the air, teaching not how to love others, but how to love only yourself. God is for everyone. *"For there is no respect of persons with God."* (Romans 2:11).

<u>**Seven Meditations For Character**</u>

"Finally, brethren, whatsoever things are true, whatsoever things are honest, whatsoever things are just, whatsoever things are pure, whatsoever things are lovely, whatsoever things are of good report; if there be any virtue, and if there be any praise, think on these things." (Philippians 4:8).

<u>*1. Things that are true*</u>

Love – It is the truest thing of all. God is love. God loves us, and he wants us to love one another. Do you know how it feels to love someone? When you love someone, it feels like no one else exists in the world, except you and that person, especially when that person feels the same. Your every thought revolves around that person, and when you are apart, there is an empty feeling deep inside of you. It is unimaginable to think of life without that person because they are a part of you. Just the thought of that person makes your heart leap. We would sacrifice anything for that person whom we love, and often make many, without second thoughts or any regrets. That is how much God loves us.

"For God so loved the world that he gave his only begotten Son, that whosoever believeth in him should not perish, but have eternal life." (John 3:16).

Sunrises – With each new sunrise, begins a brand-new day. Sunrises signify beginnings and newness. The sun raises on our lives when we are born, and when we are born again in Christ. The truth of the sunrise is in the surety of its newness. Therefore, it is in Christ as well. God promises us new hope in his word.

He promises us a new sunrise when we accept him and believe in his Son and in his word. God in his infinite wisdom, already made our sunrise when he made his Son rise.

Sunsets – Just like sunrises, sunsets are also a surety. Sunsets signify endings and finishes. They are at the end of the day and allow us to rest. We get rest from our daily chores, our tasks, our adventures, our struggles, and problems, and even from our celebrations. Sunsets are certain, and they are an end to our work. No matter when or where your sun sets, you can rest in knowing that Jesus also sits at the right hand of his Father. *"So then after the Lord had spoken unto them, he was received up into heaven, and sat on the right hand of God."* (Mark 16:19).

2. *Things that are honest*

Wisdom – Wisdom never lies. It is honest in that it does not beat around the bush with its truth. It does not sugar-coat, and it does not deceive, but it is blatantly straightforward and true in its message. If we follow wisdom, we will truly succeed, depending on how much honest effort we apply to its instruction. Wisdom has keys that unlock doors, and we are wise when we search for wisdoms keys. Wisdom is honest, it is of God, and if any of us do not have it, we should pray and ask God for it, who always gives. (James 1:5).

Work – How gratifying and satisfying it is to know that we have made a meaningful contribution through hard work. Work is honest when done, not with shortcuts or deceptions; but when done with the strength and integrity that Christ demonstrates to us in God's word. Although it may not seem so in the smallness of our minds, but to work and enjoy the fruit of our honest labor is a gift from God. (Ecclesiastes 3:13). Not only do all things work, but all things work together for good, when it is lovingly fulfilling God's purpose. (Romans 8:28).

3.Things that are just

God – because he judges us by whether we have accepted Christ, in which he has given us the freedom to choose, is just. He has given us the right to choose life in Christ, or death in the world. How much more just could anyone ever be?

"I call heaven and earth to record this day against you, that I have set before you life and death, blessing and cursing: therefore, choose life, that both thou and thy seed may live." (Deuteronomy 30:19).

Righteousness – Whatever is within the acceptable word of God is righteous, therefore, to do the righteous thing in all situations is in Christ. If we are in Christ, then we are righteous also. Judging ourselves instead of judging others is a righteous, respectable, and

Christian way for us to live. Living in judgment of others

is not for us to perform, but we should live in the Holy

Spirit as he Guides us in all truth and righteousness.

<u>**4. Things that are pure**</u>

Wind – The manifestation of the wind is eternally pure. In its substance, dwell infinite questions that have consumed man since the beginning of time. We cannot see it, but we know it is there by the way it blows. We cannot touch it, but we know exactly how it feels. We can predict when it will come, but we do not really know from where it comes. It can be gentle or harsh, hot, or cold, loud, or quiet. Within the wind, created by God in its pureness, dwell mysteries of life.

"But God remembered Noah and all the wild animals and the livestock that were with him in the ark, and he sent a wind over the earth, and the waters receded." (Genesis 8:1).

Water – Possibly the purest of all the elements, water has been here from the beginning. Pure water was here with God when he created the earth. Pure water was here with the Holy Spirit who walked upon its surface.

"And the earth was without form, and void; and darkness was upon the face of the deep. And the spirit of God moved upon the face of the waters." (Genesis 1:2).

No matter what man can dilute into it, or filter out of it, water will remain pure. For it is solid yet transparent, and impenetrable yet absorbent. Water is from God, and like him, it is life giving and life sustaining.

5. *<u>Things that are lovely</u>*

Seasons – Who can deny the beauty of the earth as it goes through its seasonal changes? The life of the earth has its seasons of transition, just as our own lives have. When looking at the earth, through sober eyes, it is easy to see the complex yet simple beauty that God has blessed us with. Even on a gloomy and stormy day (by its outward appearance), looking through the storm and beyond the gloom can reveal a loveliness all its own. Often, in the storms of our lives, we need to look through and beyond the gloom to see the loveliness of Gods purpose for our lives that is all our own. The bible says…

"He revealeth the deep and secret things: he knoweth what is in the darkness, and the light dwelleth with him. (Daniel 2:21-22).

6. Things that are of good report (admirable)

<u>Our lives</u>

"Dear friends, you are like visitors and strangers in this world. So, I beg you to keep your lives free from the evil things you want to do, those desires that fight against your true selves. People who don't believe are living all around you. They may say that you are doing wrong. So, live such good lives that they will see the good you do, and they will give glory to God on the day he comes."   (1 Peter 2:11-12) ERV.

This means that as Christians, we need to keep ourselves from doing those things that are lustful and wrong in the eyes of God. Whether they are sensual or habitual, those things go against the grain of our souls, and prevent us from being complete in our walk with

Christ. We need to not be like hypocrites, but to be the Christians that we say we are. This includes in our lifestyles as well as our conversations. Some Christians say one thing and do another or quote good scripture yet live another way that is not the way of Christ. That is why, when non-Christians see us, they often have nothing good to say because of the hypocritical stereotype that we have brought upon ourselves. When we walk with the love of God in Christ, non-Christians see us and see his light in us, which causes them to glorify God in their own ways. When we exhibit those qualities, our lives become living testimonies, admirable and of good report.

7. <u>*Things that are virtuous and praiseworthy*</u>

<u>Faithfulness and belief</u> – There are many distractions in the world today, which threaten our morality. It is only with persistence and diligence that we can maintain our faith. The bible says...

"The Lord rewarded me according to my righteousness: according to the cleanness of my hands hath he recompensed me. For I have kept the ways of the Lord and have not wickedly departed from my God." (Psalm 18:20-21).

Keeping our faithfulness to God and our belief in Jesus Christ is essential to our walk as Christians. These virtuous and praiseworthy qualities need to be part of our characters, and not just things that we have in our minds. They need to be within our hearts to become our lifestyle. Having these qualities gives glory to God and reaffirms the presence of the Holy Spirit in us by Jesus Christ our Lord and Savior.

<u>**Meditations for Peace**</u>

"Those things, which you have both learned and received, and heard, and seen in me, do; and the God of peace shall be with you."   (Philippians 4:9)

The Apostle Paul wrote the scripture to the Philippians, but we can apply this to our own Christianity, not to keep the law, because Christ already accomplished that, but to develop character. Things that we have learned and received, heard, and seen, in and during our walk with Christ and through the study of God's word, are those meditations. We know that it is not for us to judge others, but to judge ourselves to be sure that our own walk is in line with the word of God. *"You, therefore, have no excuse, you who pass judgment on someone else, for at whatever point you judge the other, you are condemning yourself, because you who*

pass judgment do the same things." (Romans 2:1 NIV).

- We know that we need to treat others with love and respect, no matter who they are, because although we are Christians, we are not perfect humans, and we too must learn as we mature in Christ.

- We know that all continue to age, but many of us never *mature*, and that is why God gives us his word through apostles, pastors, ministers, and teachers.

"To prepare God's people for works of

service, so that the body of Christ may be built up

until we all reach unity in the faith and in the

knowledge of the Son of God and become mature,

attaining to the whole measure of the fullness of Christ." (Ephesians 4:11-13).

Through God's word, we know that when we walk in the Spirit, God dwells in us. You can't just go through life with chips on your shoulder, hating everything, and dealing with people in a rude way while claiming to be a Christian. Holiness is not like a suit you can wear and change to fit the situation. It is not a pair of sandals that you slip into to walk in when the grass is green. To be Holy without thinking like we're "all that" and better than everyone else requires three things… being true to God, being true to ourselves, and being a true Christian. Amen.

NOTES

Scripture References

- ☐ 1 PETER 1:16 KJV

- ☐ MARK 10:27 KJV

- ☐ MATTHEW 6:5 NLT

- ☐ 1 PETER 3:15 KJV

- ☐ ROMANS 8:28 KJV

- ☐ JOHN 2:1-11 KJV

- ☐ PROVERBS 3:7 KJV

- ☐ PROVERBS 26:12 NLT

- ☐ MATTHEW 23:12-25 NIV

- ☐ PROVERBS 30:12 NKJV

☐ ROMANS 12:2-3 NIV

☐ GALATIANS 6:3 KJV

☐ JOHN 15:18-19 KJV

☐ ROMANS 2:11 KJV

☐ PHILIPPIANS 4:8 KJV

☐ JOHN 3:16 KJV

☐ MARK 16:19 KJV

☐ JAMES 1:5 KJV

☐ ECCLESIASTES 3:13 KJV

☐ DEUTERONOMY 30:19 KJV

☐ GENESIS 8:1 KJV

☐ GENESIS 1:2 KJV

☐ DANIEL 2:21-22 KJV

☐ 1 PETER 2:11-12 ERV

☐ PSALMS 18:20-21 KJV

☐ PHILIPPIANS 4:9 KJV

☐ ROMANS 2:1 KJV

☐ EPHESIANS 4:11-13 KJ

www.ingramcontent.com/pod-product-compliance
Lightning Source LLC
Chambersburg PA
CBHW050702250726
48662CB00002B/792